Which Is the Circle?

A BOOK ABOUT SHAPES

BY NICK REBMAN

Published by The Child's World®
1980 Lookout Drive • Mankato, MN 56003-1705
800-599-READ • www.childsworld.com

Acknowledgments
The Child's World®: Mary Swensen, Publishing Director
Red Line Editorial: Editorial direction and production
The Design Lab: Design

Photographs ©: Red Line Editorial, cover; Alena Haurylik/
Shutterstock Images, 4; Aleksandrova Karina/Shutterstock
Images, 5; Anna Yunak/Shutterstock Images, 6–7; Aniriana/
Shutterstock Images, 7; Rawpixel.com/Shutterstock Images,
8; Andrei Nekrassov/Shutterstock Images, 9; paulaphoto/
Shutterstock Images, 10; Lori Sparkia/Shutterstock Images, 11;
Lilya Espinosa/Shutterstock Images, 12; Norwalk/Shutterstock
Images, 13

ISBN 9781503807655
LCCN 2015958226

Printed in the United States of America
Mankato, MN
June, 2016
PA02306

About the Author

Nick Rebman likes to write, draw, and travel. He lives in Minnesota.

Some things are circles. Some things are squares. Can you answer these questions about shapes?

Dave is hungry. He thinks about eating pizza. Then he thinks about eating waffles.

Which is the circle?

Alice is sitting in her house. She looks at the clock. Then she looks at the window.

Which is the
square?

Tim and Maggie are on the beach.
First they see a beach ball. Then
they see the sails of a boat.

Which is the triangle?

9

Rita and William are at the bank. Rita has a dollar bill. William has a coin.

Which is the
rectangle?

Jacey is making breakfast. She has an egg. She will eat it with toast.

12

Which is the oval?

ANSWER KEY

The pizza is the circle.

The window is the square

The sails are the triangle.

The dollar bill is
the rectangle.

The egg is the oval.

GLOSSARY

circle (SUR-kull) A circle is a perfectly round shape. The pizza was a circle.

oval (OH-vull) An oval is a flattened round shape. The egg was an oval.

rectangle (REK-tang-gull) A rectangle is a shape with four sides. The dollar bill was a rectangle.

square (SKWAYR) A square is a shape with four sides that are all the same length. The window was a square.

triangle (TRY-ang-gull) A triangle is a shape with three sides. The boat's sail was a triangle.

TO LEARN MORE

IN THE LIBRARY

Evanson, Ashley. *Paris: A Book of Shapes*. New York: Grosset & Dunlap, 2015.

Pistoia, Sara. *Shapes*. Mankato, MN: Child's World, 2014.

ON THE WEB

Visit our Web site for links about shapes: **childsworld.com/links**

Note to Parents, Teachers, and Librarians: We routinely verify our Web links to make sure they are safe and active sites. So encourage your readers to check them out!

INDEX